∞∞

Papa's Portrait:

An 1820 Stephenson House

Novella

∞∞

D.L. Andersen

This book is a work of historical fiction. In order to give a sense of the times, names of real people or places as well as events have been included in the book. The story is imaginary, and the names of non-historical persons or events are the product of the author's imagination or are used fictitiously. Any resemblance of such non-historical persons or events to actual ones is purely coincidental.

In memory of

Karen Campe Matyka

1937 – 2015

CONTENTS

Acknowledgements

In the summer of 2006, I wandered into an old house, recently restored, in a community not far from where I lived. The house first caught my attention several years before when I first moved to Illinois. At that time it was a college fraternity and I had always cringed as I passed wondering at the fragile condition of this old relic and how it might be treated by the boisterous young men who lived there. Shades of *Animal House* filled my thoughts and I wondered at the house's history and how it had survived and still continued to thrive even as a college frat house. I guessed it probably dated to the 1840's by its aged brick façade and antebellum style. Yet something indefinable about the house seem to reach out and call to me every time I passed.

Sometime around the year 2000, obvious changes to the house were underway and I feared that this lovely old homestead might be slated for razing to pave the way for yet another strip mall or convenience store. To my relief I learned it was actually being renovated as a historic landmark. Local folklore had dubbed it "the Governor's House" which I was later to learn had only a partial truth to it. For the time being, I was just relieved to know a historic preservation committee had undertaken the project. Over the course of the next few years I watched with eager anticipation as each phase stripped away the years of renovations to return it to its original rustic glory. Finally the day came, I could step foot inside this house which seemed to haunt me in ways I would never have suspected at the time.

Once the project was complete, I had intended only to stop in one day for tour information or schedule a future visit. What happened next can only be attributed to the hand of some fate larger than I can fathom. I never did take that tour as a visitor and I have never since left the house without feeling like it's now my second home. Before I knew it I was filling out an application to become a volunteer "docent", a term quite new to me then but what I soon learned meant I'd be dressing the part of an 1820 woman and giving tours to others who came to visit. Over the course of the next year I met some amazing people as nuts about history and interpreting as I was. I learned a lot, laughed a lot and became increasingly enamored with the "voices" that seemed to echo from the walls, whispering their secrets, recounting stories of those who built the house and first came to Illinois territory some 160 years before I was born. The incomplete truths and partial facts incited my imagination and begged for a story to be told. When I asked if there would be a book written. I was told there one in the making. Unbeknownst to me during those years of renovation, a team of historians and researchers were hard at work behind the scenes sifting through fragmented documents, writing letters and posting queries on genealogy blogs piecing together every available detail that could be found about Col Benjamin Stephenson and his family. Among these was Karen Matyka who took on the task of writing letters in a column for the Edwardsville Intelligencer. To make the pieces of the past more engaging for the public and spur interest in the restoration, she chose a very special spokesperson to aid her cause and thus, Henry the Stephenson House Mouse was born.

Through Henry's letters written from the point of view of a mouse watching his beloved home be torn apart and rebuilt, the Edwardsville community learned of each new phase in an entertaining and lively way. At the time I met Karen, she was in the process of compiling all of the letters into a book. While I eagerly looked forward to reading her book, the wheels kept turning about plot ideas of my own for a historical fiction story about Ben and Lucy Stephenson and their adventures in early Illinois. For the first year I feared telling anyone about my ideas and tried to subtly feed suggestions to other more well connected docents and worthy researchers hoping one of them would take up the pen and write the story I wanted desperately to read.

For almost a year I hid my desire to write a book of my own, fighting character "voices" and plot ideas swirling in my head to the point of distraction. Though Karen's book remains is the best and most complete source of information in print on Benjamin Stephenson's life, and times, it didn't tell the story I had envisioned and still would not let me go. Even still, I would have given up and found a means to quiet the "voices" had it not been for Karen and a few others, who encouraged me to write my own version as a companion book for the site to offer visitors.

My first attempt was Papa's Portrait, first printed in our Volunteer Newsletter, a publication to dispense information and training for house docents. The original story was met with high acclaim, especially from Jane Denny, one of our leading researchers whose attention I was overwhelmed to have caught and whose respect I dearly coveted. But more than anyone else, I owe a debt of gratitude to Karen whose passing we mourned in February 2015. Besides giving us Henry the House Mouse who continues to delight children on school field trips, Karen offered her unswerving dedication and countless hours of research and writing to make the restored Stephenson House a landmark in our community.

However, a restoration project of this magnitude and historical fiction project to compliment it, involve a team of historically minded individuals all bringing together their talents, enthusiasm and time commitment to bring it to fruition. There are far too many others that I owe a debt of gratitude for their patient listening ears and pointing me in the right direction of information as well as bouncing all those zany plot ideas around with: site director, RoxAnn Raisner; local authors and historians, Ellen Nore, PhD and Syd Denny, PhD; genealogist, Jane Denny; fellow docents, Bob Jurgena; Elizabeth Bowling; George and Elizabeth Edwards and a host of other dedicated volunteers. But it is mostly to Karen whom we all owe a debt of gratitude, who over the years offered her friendship and quiet, gentle encouragement.

Sadly, Karen was taken from us far too soon in the wake of chronic and debilitating health issues. Through every trial, she remained a smiling irrepressible force in our historical community. I wish I had taken more time to delve into her wealth of knowledge without fear of stepping on her toes. I learned far too late she was not that sort of person. I wrongly assumed that she would be there to read and, I hoped, approve of the entire novel series I had envisioned.

It is with deep appreciation and humility, I dedicate this short story in her memory with all proceeds from sales going to a memorial fund in her honor as she would have wished. In this small way, it is my hope that others will derive some useful knowledge and understanding of her life's work and learn more about a forgotten part of America's early beginnings through the life of Colonel Benjamin Stephenson as told through the voice of his son and namesake, Benjamin Van Stephenson.

1

Edwardsville, Illinois
1819

Papa came home late again that October night, the year I turned seven. There was hardly a night I didn't remember him coming home late, but this night was different. Everyone thought I was asleep, but I wasn't. I shouldn't have been out of bed, sneaking down to the kitchen to find a morsel to eat, but that plum tart had been calling to me since suppertime. I wasn't supposed to have any, but then, I wasn't supposed to be out of bed either. At supper time, Mama wouldn't let me have dessert after I spilled my milk all over her linen table cloth and it trickled down Elvira's new silk gown. I hadn't really meant to swing my arm that hard whilst passing the bowl of greens to James.

"You've had quite enough, Benjamin Van Stephenson." I knew when Mama used my whole name I should stay out of sight for the rest of the evening. And so I did, until after the house was dark and all was quiet.

Thinking of plum tart and the empty space between my ribs kept me awake and wandering down to the kitchen. Mama was sitting on the settee in the parlor reading as I tip-toed past, quiet as could be. Once, I thought she must have heard me when the stairs creaked, 'cause she jerked her head up real sharp like. She only took a gander at the clock on the mantel. Lines puckered her forehead beneath her lace cap, the same look she gets when fussing at the servants these days, or when she is pouring over a pile of papers – her receipts as she calls them, from the shops up town.

When I knew for sure she hadn't spied me, I ducked behind the staircase and slipped real quiet into the kitchen. Sadie near made me jump out of my skin, but I stifled a yelp by biting my lower lip twixt my teeth. That ol' yellow cat paid me no mind. She sidled past me and planted herself under the table licking her paw and purring louder than a bunch of frogs in springtime at Cahokia Creek. I bent down to pet her as she passed by, rippling in a way that lets me know she likes how I scratch her from neck to tail. It reminds me of waves coursing along the river whenever she does this. I thought then about what Papa said a few weeks b ack, when he came home from St. Louis. He looked awful worried and so tired then too, just like Mama did tonight. I asked him if he had seen any of those new steamboats on the river.

He said, "One or two. Still more barges and keelboats than steamers, Little Ben." He paused and gave me a curious look. "Maybe next time I go to St. Louis, I expect you ought to go along and see for yourself. You can keep count as we cross on the ferry."

The ferry! That made me real happy 'cause when Papa makes a promise, he keeps it. I always wanted to take a ferry ride across the river. Mama says we did once when I was small and we were coming back from Washington where Pa served in congress for a few years, but I was too little to remember those days.

It's been four months, now, since Papa made that promise but I know he'll keep it in spite of what James and Elvira say. They say Papa can't always keep his promises, but I don't believe them. James is six years older than me and thinks he knows everything now that he passed his eighth level exams at the subscription school in town. Papa helped start that school with Mr. Edwards, whom I sometimes call Uncle Ninian, though he's not our real uncle. He was our first governor here in Illinois territory and the reason Papa became a sheriff. I was the only one of us kids born here in Illinois and that makes this the only home I've ever known, except for those years in Washington City, but they don't really count, since I was not yet breeched out of my baby gowns. We were just a territory then, but as of last year we became a full-fledged state, the twenty-first state to enter the Union. Maybe Uncle Ninian will be governor again someday now that we are a state rather than just a territory. Papa says he might be, and I heard he and Mama talking it about it one time. Mama says other folks say he's had his turn and should let other men take over. I wondered if Papa wanted to be governor too, but I 'spect he has enough to keep himself busy.

That's what I heard Mama say to Julia, who is a little older than James and is changing in ways that make me feel like sour apple vinegar inside. She is always talking about going to parties and balls and such and fretting over nonsense, like meeting all the proper gentlemen in town. Mama says she'll be ready next year, perhaps. Papa acts a bit grumpy and says, "Fifteen is too young to consider suitors." Mama smiles and reminds him she was younger than that when they married. I just cover my ears and go hide upstairs where I can play tin soldiers or shoot clay marbles.

At least Elvira is still willing to run and play with me outdoors. We roll hoops, play trap ball and ninepins with the sets Papa brought back from trips upriver to Louisville, Marietta and out West across to St. Louis. Once he even went all the way to New Orleans on business and brought me back a fine thaumatrope, which means "turning wheel" in some foreign tongue, according to Papa. Maybe it's Latin, or is it Greek? Papa would know, 'cause he's always reading books with big words. My thaumatrope has a red bird on one side and a cage on the other. When I spin it by the two strings looped between either side of the paper disc, it looks like the bird is in the cage, but when the disc is resting still, the bird is free once more to be on one side with an empty cage on the other. I like thinking of the bird being free, but its great sport to see him fly into his cage when I've a mind to. I wish I had a real red bird of my own, like the one that chirped outside my bedchamber window all last winter.

Thaumatrope

I thought about all this while I was getting the plum tart out of the larder box, moving slow as a barge through ice on the Mississippi so as not to alarm Sadie or bring Mama to the kitchen. Sure enough there it was, flaky and sweet and all ready for me to swallow whole, but I took my time. Instead I nibbled at the flaky crust around the edge first, before licking the gooey plum filling on top with the tip of my tongue. Papa says Winn makes the best plum tart east of the Mississippi.

I asked him once, "How about west of the Mississippi?"

He just frowned and scratched his chin like he was pondering important matters with Mr. Edwards, Mr. Pope or other gentlemen who come by his land office or meet with him in the parlor. After a pause, he turned and said, "I haven't been too far west of the Great River – yet, that is, Son. Perhaps one day I'll go clear to the Pacific Ocean, crossing every mountain, hill and valley. I'll taste all the plum tart from here to the western waters. Then I'll come back and tell you."

"If you go to the Pacific Ocean, Papa, I'm coming with you."

He laughed and said, "You have my word on that, my good man. We'll be just like Captains Lewis and Clark on the Corps of Discovery to see the Pacific Ocean." Then he held out his hand, and we shook like real gentlemen making a deal.

Papa is always making deals. That's part of his work. He makes deals with people who come to the land office to buy their homesteads here in Illinois. He also works for the bank and just this year opened a mercantile in town. One day last week I visited his shop on Main Street while he worked. A customer came into the store and asked for credit to purchase a new rake, an adze, and a sack of flour. He said he couldn't pay his past due bill since his wife had been sick of late and the crop he counted on come fall had not turned out so well. Papa gave the man a hard look, and said he couldn't extend him any more credit. He gave me a candy stick and asked me to wait outside on the porch. I was just as glad to be away from them too. I still heard them talking but not quite all the words. Later I saw Papa and his store hand, Ezra, help him load all of the things the man asked for, in the back of his wagon. The man must have found a way to pay Papa, because I know one must pay before taking things from a shop. That's what Papa and Mama always say. But when I asked later, Pa just looked more tired than I'd ever seen and said times were hard enough on folks but he had worked things out with the man, some sort of 'rangement' whatever that means.

"Not to worry, son," he said, cheerily, "I trust he'll pay in due course of time. We all have to do our part to help build our new settlement town. It took time to bring out territory to statehood, and if we're to keep growing it takes all of us working together and helping a neighbor in need now and again."

More than just making deals, Pa is also a soldier, a real colonel in the militia. I want to be a colonel, just like him someday. I was born the year the War started, the one some call the English War, or our second war for independence, and some just refer to it by the year 1812. We all lived in Prairie du Rocher near Fort Kaskaskia then. Papa says he didn't have to do much fighting, just kept the territory safe from those that might start something against us. I'm glad of it, though if I were in a war, I'd sure want to do some fighting. Maybe someday I'll get that chance too.

The door latch clicked. At first I was afraid someone was coming into the kitchen, so I ducked under the table. But it wasn't the kitchen door that creaked. Instead it was the front door. Then I heard Papa's footsteps and Mama meeting him in the entryway.

"Ben, it's about time you got home. Do you know how late it is?" Mama's voice sure sounded like it did when she scolded me at dinner, but this time it was Papa getting the tongue lashing.

I moved toward the kitchen door and peeked out, bracing one foot ready to pull back if I was seen. They stood at the other end of the hall by the front door. Mama held the collar of his greatcoat while Papa slipped his arms out of the snug sleeves.

"Lucy, don't start this now. I should be at the office still, but I couldn't bear another dot or squiggle of that ledger anymore. Deeds, accounts, legal drafts. I've had enough for one day's work." Papa sighed and sat down on the hall seat to take off his boots. His shoulders hunched over and his face was pinched and sad. "I've got an early meeting tomorrow with the board. There's enough to give an accounting for now. Perhaps that will appease them."

"You aren't the only one who's responsible for all of this. That bank. The land office. What next? What have the rest to say for it all?" Mama brushed off his greatcoat and hung it on the hall tree. "Can't someone else work out the books too? Manage the affairs? You can only be expected to do so much in one day, between the bank and the land office. "

Pa let out a slow breath like the sound of the tea kettle whistling on the hearth. "Well, m'dear, it all comes with being the bank president, you know. At least you can be if glad the mercantile doesn't pan out as hoped."

"Don't you put all that on me." Mama spoke soft with a slight waver in her throat like a tea kettle losing its steam. "I never said as much, and you well know it."

"You didn't have to," Pa muttered, "I've known your sentiment on it all along."

Mama set the hat alongside his coat and turned on her heels. "Meet with the board, indeed. What's brewing now? More of Edwards' schemes again? Surely not more trouble with Secretary Crawford. There've been more foreclosures as well? I heard about the Bartletts at our Sunday School Society meeting today. You can't let them lose their home, Ben."

"Nothing to worry about dear," Papa said, "Ultimately I'm responsible for all the dealings between the bank and the land office, but it's nothing we can't manage. The Board may hold sway but I'm still president. I'm doing everything I can to extend loans, avoid foreclosures, particularly for those we are on friendly terms with. You think I like how things are? However, times being what they are, people are unable to pay their loans for the land. The government expects payment in due course of time. It's why I'm appointed both land agent and bank president. To see the job is done, land is sold and payment is rendered in full. They well knew as much when they signed for the loans."

"Still, I say it's too much for you. And times being what they are…"

"… folks are unable to pay their loans," Papa finished her thought, "Yes, I'm well aware of this, m'dear. Not that hard cash has ever been in plentiful supply out here."

"Isn't there something you could do? Surely they could pay what they can and..."

"And what?" Pa laughed, not in any merry sort of way, but in a hard, cold way that made me shiver. "I can't very well send a hog or a hogshead of whisky back east as payment. You know a man came in today wanting to pay his loan with his young slave girl instead."

"What?" Mama clasped a hand to her throat. "That's illegal now that we're a free state."

"So long as the indentures are still in force, they can be sold, free state or not. It's moot anyway. Congress doesn't want to deal with the sale of slaves as government revenue. It's gold and silver specie they hanker for from land sales to build government coffers."

One boot was off, then the other, and he slipped on his red leather house shoes Mama gave him last Christmas. Pa looked more at ease as he spoke now. "It will indeed mean more foreclosures to come, if conditions don't change. I'm doing all I can to help those in need keep their farms, extending loans, allowing them to pay whatever they can muster up. But there are limits, legal conditions to meet." He leveled his hands in the air as if holding everything and nothing all together. "There is only so much I can do, sweetheart."

"The Bartletts, Ben." Mama held a hand against her cheek. "They've been good friends, decent, hard working people and with another baby on the way..."

"Another letter from Crawford arrived today" - Papa voice dropped low – "requiring payment for the government land sales be sent post haste. With all the banking scandals these days, counterfeit currency, bank closings, there's more talk about my being both receiver of public monies as well as bank president."

"As if that's your fault, is it now?" Mama declared. "As I recall

President Madison approved your appointment and with a glowing recommendation from the esteemed Mr. Edwards. He was more than pleased with your work then. You've distinguished yourself as sheriff, keeping the peace among French, American, Kickapoo and other tribes... Your service in the War... Does that count for nothing? And this Secretary Crawford. Wasn't it he that encouraged you to set up the bank here in Edwardsville, specifically to hold the land office money in one safe depository?"

"My thoughts as well." His hands spread open like trying to hold water in a sieve. "But 'tis Washington bureaucracy at work. My dual roles do appear a conflict of interest. A bit of the ol' fox watching the henhouse."

"Ben, you are not some treacherous fox watching a henhouse and they should well know it."

"As it is, the Missouri Territory banks are raising issue again, trying to undercut our system here any way they see fit." Papa stood and stretched to his full height. He's only a smidgeon above Mama, but he looks so tall and strong when he stretches up like that. His arms reached around and held her close.

"Well, Ninian Edwards can surely help out too." Mama laid her head on Papa's shoulder, muffling her voice into his woolen coat. "He's the one who insisted you accept the office of Receiver as well as the bank president position. I told you three years ago after you left your post in Congress, I feared it would be too much for all of us, especially for your health. You'll wear yourself into an early grave, especially with the fever seasons coming like they do out here."

"Well, what would you have us do, m'dear?" Papa was sounding testy again, like Mama did at supper time. "Shall we move back to Virginia? Are the fevers any more tolerable back there? Should we have kept your father's land and settled down to farming? Would there have been enough land to pass on to our boys when they grew to men?

Should I have stayed a deputy sheriff in Harper's Ferry? Do you want to start that tack again?"

"That's not what I'm saying at all." Mama's voice matched Pa's testiness now, like she sounds when she is scolding one of us for playing too rough or getting in the servants way and not minding our manners. Her voice smoldered down to ash, soft and whispery. "The children almost never see you anymore."

I saw by the look on Papa's face he didn't like being told this, not one bit, though he said nothing, only held her close, hands fisted against the small of her back. He pulled her face up to his, and their lips met. I don't like it when they do that, so I looked away real quick and watched Sadie scurry after a mouse over the bricks of the hearth and into the corner.

When Papa spoke again, I knew it was safe to look, so I peeked back out into the hall. "Edwards is resigning from the board. He told me this morning. Said he'll have his official notice on my desk tomorrow early. It'll be in the papers soon after. Warren will see to that, I'm sure."

"What? Is that what all this is about? Hooper Warren has another reason to sell more newspapers at your expense? Another reason to attack you with calumny. He's supposed to be your friend, even if his views--"

"Now, Lucy." Papa stroked the back of her neck, the way I pet Sadie when she's scared or fidgety. "It's business. We are fortunate to have a solid newspaper like *The Spectator* in these parts. There is no personal assault to be made. I take no offense to it and neither should you. Warren and I are on good terms, as ever."

"Nevertheless,the board meeting. Your penchant for working late every night. And that's how they all thank you?" Mama gasped and pulled out of Papa's hold. "Ninian of all people can't do this. It was him that got you into this mess and now he leaves you to clean up afterward?" A fine thing for someone who calls you a friend. And after all you've done for him, with the militia and political stumping, not to mention your work as sheriff, territorial representative and framing the constitution without even so much as a vote in Congress."

"Now, dear, you give me far too much credit. I do understand his reasons. It's business. And you well know we've prospered under his connections as much as we've helped his political gain."

"Ben," Mama said in a quivering breath, like the downdraft coming from the hearth just then. "Maybe it is high time we think of moving back. My cousin, Thomas, Uncle Swearingen, between them they'd find a good position for you. We'd be away from here, among family again."

Papa stepped back, tilted her chin up and leaned in close. "You'd really want that? Leave all we have here? All we've built together? Fought for? Even that new brick house of yours you've been eager to live in?"

"We'd be away from here. It wouldn't matter so much. We could sell the land, the house could be rebuilt anywhere, it isn't so far along we couldn't pull up stakes and start over again. And it would be better for you. Your health. Sell it all, and the land. I don't much care anymore."

"You're tired. We all are, but things will improve. We can't give up." He chuckled, not so like before but in his old merry way, before kissing the tip of her nose. You know I'd have never gotten this far, even with your family's connections. I could be happy anywhere so long as you and the children are there. But think on it. Leave Edwardsville? Could you truly do that? You love your work with the Sunday School Society, the Singing Society," he said, "And what happened to those dreams you have of seeing all our slaves gain their freedom? We'd have to take them all back with us. Their indentures could be revoked and we'd have no recourse but to legally keep them in bondage. We promised never to sell them. Yet we can't afford to free them and help them make a decent start. Would you really want to chance all that?"

"You're the one who voted to keep our territory a slave state. I'll have you know, and against the tenets of the Northwest Ordinance, no less." Mama pulled away, hands on her hips.

"Yes, a politician must make deals with the Devil. You know how that goes as well as anyone."

"Perhaps. But I do what I can for all of them, paltry as it may seem. The Sunday School Society does fine work educating both the poor white children and the children of color, slave or free. I've never made any pretense of that. And I will see they all get the best chance they can, regardless."

"Yes, sweetheart, and in Virginia you think you'd have such opportunities? The laws there forbid even the teaching of reading to slaves or freemen of color."

"Perhaps things could change there as well. Couldn't they?" She cocked her head at Papa, just the way Julia does whenever that Daniel Tolman comes around to work on plans for the new house.

"No, my love." Now it was Papa's turn to whisper gently into her ear. "Illinois is where our home is now and for our bondsmen as well, until such time as conditions are better for us all."

"I don't know. I'm not saying I much like how things are. I don't have all the answers either."

"Then what are you saying exactly? Do you truly wish to leave or shall we stay the course, see this through and bring our dreams to fruition."

"Perhaps. Still I don't like the sound of it." Mama clasped her hands at the high waistline of her gown. "You'd have done well for yourself and we'd have prospered no matter what, perhaps better without the aid of our dear Governor –"

"Senator Edwards, now, my sweet," Papa corrected.

"Yes, indeed. Senator Edwards," She mocked, teasingly. "Still, I can't abide the conditions of the slaves back in Virginia, let alone those horrible stories told further South. Here at least there is hope, perhaps for all of us."

"Edwards' reasons for leaving the bank's board of directors extends beyond our situation." Papa leaned against the hall tree, running a finger down the smooth wood grain. "He'll be spending most of his time with his new appointment with frequent trips to Washington over the next year or so. He still has hopes for the ambassadorship to Mexico."

"Oh, that again? Yes, quite the feather in his cap that will be." Mama turned away from Papa and looked down the hall so her eyes peered on the kitchen door, sharp as a cat's. I thought for sure she would see me so I pulled back into the darkness of the corner and held my breath. I wanted to hear more, especially now they were talking about Uncle Ninian. If they found me, I'd have to return to bed, and probably get a whipping as well.

She started down the hall toward the kitchen. My heart beat loud in my chest; I feared she would know I was there. With a swish of her skirts she veered toward the door of the parlor. "I thought he had his hat set on the governorship again. It wasn't enough for him to be territorial governor. No, he has to be governor now that Illinois officially is a state. What next? President of the United States?"

"Perhaps," Papa stood behind her with his hands on her shoulders. " But only after he goes to Mexico as an ambassador." Both my parents laughed. It was good to hear them laugh. I held my hand firm against my mouth so I wouldn't laugh too.

"Imagine the connections we could have then," Papa said, "He's a statesman, groomed for a life in politics. You know that as well as anyone. 'Tis all the business of politics."

"And he's seen fit to drag you along too, it would seem. To clean up his messes at every turn, no less. Do his bidding. And leave you high and dry." Mama turned and pressed her back against the door frame. Her voice quieted; her lip trembled. Even from where I crouched behind the door in the shadows, holding the edge of the door, I knew it was a tear she brushed from her cheek. "Ben, whatever shall we do? The house — will it be beyond our means now?"

"A moment ago you were wanting to sell it lock, stock and barrel and move back east," Papa teased. "Now you do wish to stay, is it? Ah! Tis a mere trifling, a bump in our road. We shall endeavor to persevere." He stood tall, with a finger pointed high, as if he were stumping for his position in Congress again. His voice boomed across the hallway. "Unless the Lord buildeth the house, they that labor, labor in vain." He held a hand to his chest, his voice like a preacher at a Camp Revival.

"And it is vain that you rise up early and go late to rest," Mama continued the verse, " Eating the bread of anxious toil." She threw up her hands dismissively.

I should have known from which Bible book they were quoting, but at the moment I couldn't recall just which one. A Psalm I think, or was it from Proverbs?

"Oh, Ben, that'll be quite enough." She playfully slapped him as he reached his long arms around her again.

Papa's face brightened; he raised his hand to her face. "I promised you a fine house, and a fine house you shall have, fine as any we saw back in Maryland or Virginia. I stopped by to see the progress this afternoon after dinner at the tavern. Within the year, you shall be quite the fine lady of the manor." His voice was merrier than before, like the sound of a flock of birds in springtime or streams of water rushing into the rain barrel. He lifted Mama by her waist and twirled her around.

"Oh, we'll get through this somehow, Madame. I've been through worse disasters than this, and so have you."

"Benjamin, stop this minute." Mama stifled a squeal that turned into muffled laughter, buried in Pa's sturdy shoulder. Her feet skimmed above the floor as he whirled her in his arms. "The children, Ben. And the servants. You'll waken them. What will they think?"

"Well, madame, they shall see their mother and mistress of the house is not the fuss budget she has been of late." He stopped twirling her but still held her close. "There's no sense in fretting over all of this, my love. It won't add one iota to your life, and it only makes troublesome lines on that pretty face of yours."

Papa always says that to Mama. I was thinking, too, just how pretty Mama was when Sadie skittered past under my feet. Through the narrow opening of the kitchen door she fled. I lost all bearing, so surprised was I, that I fell forward and crashed into the hallway. Sadie hissed and fled up the stairs, leaving me alone to face my doom. I couldn't breathe. My hands stung from the slap against the hard wood. My chest ached with the loss of breath. My eyes adjusted to the pain and darkness to see Papa's two red mules under my nose. One tapped a steady beat like a drum marching soldiers into battle. Mama's lavender silk hemline billowed over my hands as she bent to help me up.

"Benjamin Van Stephenson, what are you doing up so late?" Her voice sounded cross, but her hands were soft and gentle as they lifted me from the hard floor, brushing off my robe and pressing a cool hand to my heated cheek. "And just look at your face. You've been nipping some of Winn's plum tart, haven't you? And after I told you no dessert." She licked her fingers and rubbed them hard against my sticky chin.

"I... I'm sorry, Ma'am. Sir." I looked up to see Papa's unreadable glare. Did he look at his men in the militia that way, I wondered? He sometimes spoke to James and me as if we were his soldiers, too. I always liked this, but just now, I wasn't so sure.

"Well, what have we here?" Papa looked down from way above me, his arms crossed over his chest. "A spy infiltrating our ranks, is it? Harboring contraband? And out of his quarters past curfew? Soldier, what have you to say for yourself?"

"I... I'm sorry sir," I mumbled, my heart pounding louder than ever. "I was a bit hungry from dinnertime."

His mouth twitched and he stroked his chin. "You know, I was thinking a bit of plum tart sounds mighty good about now. Private Stephenson, would you care to join me for a ration of pie and fillee of milk before seeking our quarters for the night?"

"Yes, sir." I saluted.

2

Edwardsville, Illinois
1822

The October wind whistled around the eaves of the big brick house.
We'd lived just outside Edwardsville for almost a year now, since last
December when our new house was finally completed. It was three
years ago when I sat in the old kitchen in our house behind the land
office, eating plum tart with Father. I've passed ten winters now, and
much too old to be caught sneaking down to the kitchen at night for
sweets, yet I can't help remembering that last time I shared a moment
alone with my father, nibbling the crumbs of Winn's plum tart and
drinking down a cold mug of milk.

A candle burned in his bedchamber, though it was late into the
night. I heard Mama stirring, coupled by Father's fevered groans.

"I'll get the elixir, Ben," Mother's voice sounded worried again, but
efficient and in control. "Here, take this till I return with the yellow bark
tea. You need your rest."

Father had been groaning a lot these days and holding his head
with a pained look. He sometimes forgot where he put things or
mumbled as if he saw things none of us could see and shivered as if it
were the dead of winter. Elvira said, "It's the fever and ague, again."

I said to her, "What's arguing got to do with fever? Arguing don't
make you sick and cause a fever."

She shook her head at me and said I was too young to understand.

I said she was only a girl, and how would she know? I was going to be one of Father's soldiers someday and girls can't be soldiers. Elvira sat up in bed, her knees clutched to her chest, and stared. I stood at our bedchamber door looking across the hall where the candle light wavered on the bedside table in Father's room. It cast strange misshapen shadows across the wall. A distorted profile of Papa's chiseled face shook against the mantle and splashed across the wing chair where he always like to read before bedtime.

Mother saw me standing in the doorway. "Why are you children still up? Your father is ill and needs his rest. He doesn't need to hear you arguing."

I told her what Elvira said, and Mother's brows knitted a moment as if she hadn't heard me. A slight smile crinkled the corners of her mouth, leaving dimples that Father said were the reason he married her. Then he'd wink at Mama and she would blush.

Another racking cough from Father diverted Mother's attention a moment. She bit her lip and looked back toward the bed where Papa lay. Between labored breaths he coughed and moaned. The shadowy forms shook and split into fitful demons arguing around the room.

"Is it the arguing that gave Papa the fever?" I thought about how much arguing I had heard between our parents in the past three years. Arguments about money, about Papa's work, the new house, the bank and Uncle Ninian, whom everyone else called Senator Edwards, but to me he was always Uncle Ninian, even if he was too busy to come around much these days. He and Father had an argument some weeks back over something that still puzzles me. I tried asking Mother, but it only made her turn away with moist eyes. She told me to go out and play and never say more about it. But I suppose if I think on it now, it won't be so bad. Maybe when Father is well again, I'll ask him. I had stopped by Father's office one day after school and waited in the outer room while he spoke with Uncle Ninian.

"Edwards, I told you, it's dishonest. I won't be party to fraud."

"Now, Stephenson, it isn't fraud, exactly," Uncle Ninian said. "Don't think of it like that. A letter stating it wasn't our doing to put you in both offices simultaneously will be to our benefit. It's based in truth."

"Based in truth, is not the same as telling the truth," Father retorted, "And you damn well know it. We both knew the risks at the time. I agreed to both offices and in both offices I will remain, seeing this through. Stating otherwise now…"

"We knew nothing of the sort. Not that we'll admit to. It's Crawford's doing. He allowed this, endorsed it with Madison's approval as well and now he'll try to weasel out of it. Mark my words on this. We've only a little time to act before…"

"I said no," Father said. "And that's final. I see no call for it. What will it prove?"

"A great deal," Uncle Ninian retorted, "All we need is a letter stating as such. I won't allow him to leave us as his convenient scapegoats. The Missouri banks are closing in. We've only a little time now."

"You've resigned your position." The squeak of Father's chair indicated he stood, and his footsteps rounded the desk. I hid further behind the book case in the outer office. "You've made your point. This is my hand to play now, Edwards."

"The point is…"

"No, that is the point." Father's voice sounded like nails grating against rock. "We can fight this, legally. Weather it through on our own terms. We have nothing to hide, or at least I don't."

"Just what do you mean by that?" Uncle Ninian slammed down his hand on the desk. I had peeked around the corner just in time and then shrank back behind the tall secretary in the front office.

"It's Crawford's doing, as you say," Father levied back. "And Crawford will suffer the consequences for it, or work it out to the good of all. We've nothing to hide. I've tried to run an honest bank, kept an accurate accounting of all our dealings. There still may be time to recover the loss, balance the books…"

A deathly silence followed that chilled my skin into goose flesh, even though I wasn't quite sure why. At last Uncle Ninian spoke through gritted teeth like the good Reverend Schoolmaster does when about to scold one of the unruly boys in class. "Stephenson, you know the situation with the bank, the precarious place we are in. The Missouri banks are closing in as we speak. The money is no more. The funds Crawford is asking for, do you have them? Should the St. Louis banks cash out their bonds, what then? The counterfeit currency is everywhere, too much to track, even for you, diligent though you may be. There is no saving it now. Kane, Pope and the rest are out to see us ruined. If you write this letter, it may save at least our future interests and anything else that may be at stake. We can each walk away clear of it all, our heads held high."

"You mean it will save your precious political career." Father sat at his desk, his hand bracing his head. "I've no more interest in politics. I'll face the consequences as they come and hold my head high over it all."

Uncle Ninian snorted. "What else will you do? Run a shop to earn back the money should the bank collapse? That will take more than a lifetime, especially in this economy and with your business sense. You've that newly built house to fund. I could help you defray the cost, pay off the creditors. Make it far grander than those plans you've drawn up. Just name your price."

"Edwards, I don't want your money. I'll earn it myself, in time. Recoup the loss for our personal interests. There still is time for that at least. Surely, when all is said and done, Crawford will see the sense in it. If my resignation is called for, then so be it. I've nothing to hide and there still may be time to reverse this situation, should circumstances improve for the nation and the state."

"Perhaps there is, but perchance there is not." He leaned over the desk toward Father. "Do you really want to take that chance? It could mean bankruptcy, scandal, prison, even. Do you really want to put Lucy and the children through all that?"

"We'll take whatever comes and weather it through. We always have. I've done no wrong here."

More words were muttered that I didn't really understand, about banking, interests, letters, and the like. Men's names I'd never heard of before. Father knows so many people. I didn't really pay mind to it then. I wished they would stop arguing. In the end, Uncle Ninian stormed out of the office, past me hiding behind the secretary as if he didn't even see me. But Papa's keen eye caught me when he came out into the front office. That was the first time I noticed how pale and haggard he looked.

Over the next few weeks, his fever worsened until now it kept Mother and me awake standing, there in the hallway between the bedchambers. "It's the arguing that gave Papa a fever, isn't it? I asked again.

Mama looked at me for a moment as if I weren't even there. Then she walked forward and placed a hand on my shoulder. "Your Father is very ill. He has the ague, which some folks call swamp fever and some call malaria. It's got nothing to do with arguing, Son. It's just the way things are."

Mother's hand pressed into my shoulder as if to steady her stance. She swayed hesitantly before leaning forward to seal warm lips against my forehead. When she stepped back, her eyes were pools of water, shining in the star-filled night, reflecting off the hall windows against the candlestick in her hand.

"Doctor Todd will be here in the morning. Now try to get some sleep."

A week later Papa was dead. Mother made sure he had the grandest funeral that befit a statesman who had signed the Illinois Constitution, served in Congress and earned the rank of Colonel during the War of 1812. I didn't care one hoot about all the people who came, the fancy caisson that carried his body to the burial, while we walked behind, or the brick-lined grave Mother ordered to serve as his final resting place. I just kept remembering the promise Papa made that one day he returned from St. Louis and I asked about the steamboats. One day we would travel all the way to the Pacific Ocean, but that would never be now. He would never stand with me where Captains Lewis and Clark first stood and proclaimed "Ocean in view. Oh! The joy!"

Where was Papa now? The preacher said he was in some distant land where all would be made right. Did he see a magnificent ocean? Were there mountains grander than the ones he longed to see out west? Thinking on this made my eyes melt into pools of water like I'd seen in Mama's weary face some nights ago. Here she stood, not a tear shed, between my sisters on a cold October day, all of them in their black bombazine and crepe. Such silly words women gave for a dreary fabric to mourn the dead.

I would not cry. I was one of Father's soldiers and man of the house, now that James would soon be leaving for college. I would take care of Mother in the red brick house that Papa had worked so hard to build for us.

A few weeks later a man came to inventory everything in the house. I didn't like the look of him. Mother said I must be polite and act a gentleman as befits a Stephenson. She wouldn't say why every candlestick and dish had to be placed dutifully on a list, but James knew. I wondered if it had anything to do with Father's last argument with Uncle Ninian about the bank. I had heard that strange word again , the one he uttered to Father those weeks ago in his office – bankruptcy. It was whispered again between Mother and the man now sitting at Father's secretary, counting everything in our house from ink bottle to Father's precious books. Uncle Ninian had come to the funeral and told Mother he'd be there to help with the arrangements, assemble his papers and handle something he called Father's 'personal effects." He seemed eager to sort through Papa's office, making me wonder about the things I heard that day. Would he find the letter he needed? Did Father leave it for him there? I knew that must be what he wanted, but I didn't tell anyone. What did it matter? It would not bring my Papa back, and that was all I really wanted right then.

"They're going to auction everything in the house," James said, while the man sat fingering every item Mother showed him. "We're poor as church mice now. Father left us in debt." His lip curled and he spat out 'Father' as if it were our Papa's fault for dying and leaving us alone and in want. "The creditors are coming to take everything. We may even lose the house."

"No!" I stamped my foot and clenched my fists. I wanted to pound them into James's face. "They can't have Papa's house. It's our house now. He built it for us."

James just shrugged and said, "It's the law."

"Well I hate the law, and I hate this town, and the bank for killing Papa, and taking his money." I didn't care who heard me. "And Uncle Ninian too, for allowing it to happen and quitting the bank." I wasn't sure about this last part. I probably shouldn't have said it, not while the strange man was here taking what James called an "inventory" of all our household goods to sell at auction. Mama's fine china, our beds and every chair. Papa's fine books he always read to us. Even the candlesticks and Mama's pretty glassware we brought out for company and Sunday suppers. I thought about my marble collection and the tin soldiers Papa had given me from when he was a little boy. Would they take those too?

Mother stood at the dining room door giving me a hard look. The man had finished his inventory. He, stared at me too. His pudgy face resembled a pig's rosy jowls and pug nose; heavy eyes peered at me over gold rimmed spectacles. "I'll review the list, Mrs. Stephenson, and do what I can to assist your situation. It will all go to probate now. I do think we've enough to manage for the time being." He winked at her in a curious way. "I shall return Wednesday, next. I do wish there was more I could do."

He turned to leave out the front door, his heels clicking across the hardwood planking.

That night before bed, Mother called me into the parlor. She sat with a miniature portrait of Father in her hands. Her slender fingers traced the outline of the gold frame around painted ivory. I had seen it only once before on Mother's chest of drawers and knew the story well but I listened as she told it to me once again.

"Your father gave me this miniature many years ago. He had been away for a while on a long business trip down south. He sat for a portrait artist while in New Orleans one summer. It's not nearly as handsome as I recall him then." She sighed and her hand fingered the onyx broach at her throat. She nodded toward the portrait now cradled in her lap. "I was so very young then, but still I hoped he would return to marry me someday as he had promised once. And eventually he did."

"I want you to have this to remember your father. He will always be with us through you and this portrait."

"Won't it be part of the things to be auctioned?" I asked, wondering who would get Papa's portrait and why should they want it more than we did?

Mother shook her head and smoothed a hand down her dark skirt. "No, not everything will have to go. Mr. Curtis promised me we could keep a few things we need and a few precious things that mean more to us than any price could bring." She looked at me hard, her mouth compressed into a thin line. "And we'll be able to keep the house. James should not have told you what he did. It's mine now and no one can take that from us until I say so. That's the law.

I was glad to hear that. "Father wanted to go west. He wanted to see the mountains and the ocean, "I said, "I was going to go with him someday."

Mother smiled, and her mouth twitched as if she were swallowing something hard, an un-chewed bit of biscuit. That's how my throat felt. I wondered if hers did too?

"Your father wanted to do many wonderful things. He did do a great deal of important things, though mostly with others in mind, and never a thought for himself. In the summer of 1803, he had the chance to sail with the Corps of Discovery. But we'd recently married, and our Julia would be born that fall. And so he stayed behind, to tend his family and missed his great adventure.

"I want to go west someday and see a territory made into a state, and fight as a soldier and have a great adventure." I stood tall and tried to make my voice sound like Papa's that night he stood in the hallway with Mother and spoke like a great preacher, or when he ordered me and James about like we were his soldiers.

Mother looked a bit startled, as if something reminded her of a time long forgotten. Did she think I sounded too much like Papa? I didn't want to ask, but I hoped I did sound like him, just a bit.

"I'm certain you shall do many grand things to make us all proud," she said, "You will leave this house someday, though not too soon, I pray. And when that time comes, I hope you will always keep your father's portrait with you, and carry his memory wherever you may be."

She stood and pressed my father's portrait into my hand before she added a final thought.

"Then no matter where you go, he will always be there and perhaps you will fulfill the dreams he never had the chance to achieve, and perchance, many more adventures of your own in the making."

3

California
1850

Years later, I stood on the top of a mountain overlooking the Pacific Ocean. California, soon to become a state, was still in the midst of a frenzied gold rush. A different kind of fever and ague affected the people here. The fever and quaking need to gain wealth and power, not much different than those days back in old Illinois. I've seen men gain untold riches overnight and lose more than the worth of my father's bank in one wrong turn of a card hand. Still, I never forgot the words my Mother told me that day the lawyer came to inventory our family's goods.

A few months before I left for California, Mother had gone to be with Papa. I stayed, as Father would have wanted, to be with her in those last agonizing days of her illness, before making my trek westward. My older brother James had passed on a few years earlier, from the wasting sickness just after resigning from the governor's race that year. My two sisters have families of their own to tend back in Illinois. And so, it was left to me to fulfill Father's legacy.

I've done well in California and seen many wondrous things. My business ventures have prospered since leaving Illinois, though I can't say I'm all that wealthy, and somehow that doesn't matter so much. I've learned and seen far more, no amount of silver or gold could measure. I remember my parents words echoing through the years. Through the arguing, the fears and doubts, they never gave up on each other, on dreams, on all of us and never on this new land, this new nation, they helped shape. It has all brought me to this one moment. All of the gold in the California hills pales in comparison to the feeling of standing on a mountain top overlooking the Pacific Ocean, my father's portrait in hand.

"Ocean in view. Oh! the joy!"

4

_____

Author's Note

_____

In 1976 a woman entered a stamp and coin shop in Carmel, California. In her hand she bore a box of odds and ends she wanted to sell. Seeing that the box contained some interesting Cuban stamps, the dealer, Major Gary Starkey, purchased the box for $50. Later he discovered one curious item at the bottom – a miniature watercolor on ivory portrait measuring only 2- 7/8 X 2- 1/8 inches and bearing the likeness of a Regency era gentleman. The fact that the portrait was encased in a fine gold frame intrigued Starkey more than knowing more about the early 19th century gentleman portrayed with an enigmatic half smile. He took it to a local museum to discover its worth and was told to consult the Smithsonian which might be interested in the find for its newly created collection of early American miniature portraits. Upon examination, the Smithsonian verified its authenticity and estimated a value of $600.

At the time, little was known about the portrait or its origin, other than it carried the provenance of being an early American gentleman- Colonel Benjamin Stephenson. The shop owner must have wondered who this man was and what his knowing smile meant. After some consideration, he decided to donate the portrait to the Smithsonian Art Institute in Washington, D.C., where it remains to this day. In the intervening years it sat silently and patiently waiting for the day it would be rediscovered and shared with the world. That day came in June 2003 during an internet search for more information on the Stephenson family as the historic restoration project was underway.

This single portrait of Colonel Benjamin Stephenson, became a guiding force in piecing together the restoration of the home, as well as an impetus to the fictional story presented here. The house Ben and Lucy discuss building in the story still stands today nearly 200 years later, welcoming visitors to its doors and offering a living history hands-on experience for all ages to explore the past. To this day no one knows how the portrait found its way to the western shores of California in a cigar box filled with Cuban stamps. Who the woman was that sold the box to the dealer, and how she came by it, also remains a mystery.

One theory is based on the fact the younger son, Benjamin V. Stephenson, did indeed migrate to California in 1850, just after his mother's death and possibly for business opportunities in the wake of the 1849 Gold Rush. My fictional version presented here takes it one step further to explore those final tumultuous years of Col. Stephenson's life in detail, as he worked to build both a permanent home for his family and add another state to the growing Union. The conclusion of the story offers one fanciful motivation for the portrait's ultimate journey westward in the hands of the younger Benjamin Stephenson. The portrait and the lives of the Stephenson family are filled with many such unsolved mysteries that continue to intrigue and incite the imagination of visitors who come to experience a forgotten piece of America's past.

Original water color on ivory portrait of Col. Benjamin Stephenson, circa 1800

Courtesy of the Smithsonian Art Institute

The Stephenson's journey to Illinois began in 1809 when Ben and Lucy arrived with their three young children: Julia (age 5), James (age 3) and Elvira (an infant born only a few months earlier in Kentucky). Our protagonist for this story, young Benjamin V, would be born in 1812 in Illinois territory. In the coming years, the elder Benjamin would distinguish himself as a territorial county sheriff, a militia officer during the War of 1812, and a US. Congressman, taking him back east to Washington City for two terms before returning to his beloved Illinois. By 1816 he received an appointment from President Madison as Receiver of Public Monies and set up a land office in the burgeoning frontier town of Edwardsville, IL.

The sole purpose of the land office was to sell off tracts of land as homesteads in the fertile river valleys that give credence to Illinois as

"The Prairie State". At the time the territory was better known as The Land of Goshen – an appellation given by early settlers as comparison to the Promised Land of Biblical fame. Many songs of the era spurred people onward to this new land, such as *Bound for the Promised Land* and *Ellanoy*, both which spoke metaphorically of a fertile land of rivers and valleys akin to the fertile crescent and Nile River valley of Egypt where God's chosen people were blessed and prospered.

Indeed, many at the time came flocking to the lower Illinois bottoms between the Ohio and Mississippi Rivers and Ben Stephenson had his work cut out for him. In order to safeguard the money earned from land sales, before sending it off to Washington, a suitable depository for the funds was needed. Congress approved the charter for The Bank of Edwardsville. Secretary of the Treasury, William Crawford, appointed Stephenson as president of the bank, which, as the story shows here, would prove problematic in the coming years.

In the meantime, the family prospered and gained social prominence among the Edwardsville community. Lucy served as secretary of both a Sunday School Society and a Singing Society, while also performing duties as wife to a territorial politician and gentleman banker as well as mother to a growing family. She must have played hostess to many parties and social gatherings where her distinguished husband presided. And, as the story indicates, there must also have been many late nights and lengthy travels that separated the couple, leaving Lucy alone to tend the children with the aid of the servants they brought into the territory as slaves. The issue of slavery was a contentious and controversial subject that was only hinted at in this story, but will be dealt with in more detail in an upcoming full-length novel about the Stephenson family.

The year 1818 proved to be a watershed moment for Stephenson and his family, as an economic collapse wreaked havoc with settlers strapped with loans for land in a system with little cash flow and a banking system not FDIC insured. In spite of what appear to be Stephenson's valiant efforts, the bank failed right in the midst of building what is presumed to be their "dream home" – the fulfillment of their years of struggle and frequent relocation from Virginia to Kentucky to finally, Illinois. It was here in this new home, he perhaps hoped to see his children raised, eventually marry, and ultimately live a life of ease and affluence, growing old with his beloved wife, Lucy.

Like the fictional version here indicates, there was friction and political unrest between territorial Governor Ninian Edwards, close friend and ally to Stephenson, and several political factions. Edwards did, in fact, resign from the bank's Board of Directors in 1819 amidst banking troubles and economic turmoil, presumably to save face and his political career. How this sat with Stephenson and what affect it had on their friendship is unknown, however, we can only imagine there might have been some friction between them, not to mention the tensions it must have brought to bear on Stephenson's own marriage and household. Unfortunately, the historical record is silent on that subject and all that remains are bare bones facts, from which I've strived to tell a story of family, not unlike today, struggling to hold everything together in the face of hard economic times and a struggling Federal reserve.

Like a scene straight out of a Dickens' novel, Stephenson faced a horrific banking loss, public scandal and an untimely death due to some sudden illness that befell him in the fall of 1822, a mere nine months after finishing the house that still stands today. It's believed he died of malaria, then known by an assortment of names as Lucy lists in the story: fever and ague, swamp fever, bilious fever. Malaria was pandemic on the Midwestern frontier, particularly in the muggy Mississippi Valley, still known today for its hot humid summers and hordes of mosquitoes.

Today medical experts recognize the mosquito as the culprit for carrying the parasite that infects the blood stream. There it remains dormant until triggered by the circadian rhythm of a person's body and recurs as intermittent fevers, ultimately attacking the liver and other vital organs. Whether Stephenson was plagued by these remittent fevers or suffered only one fatale bout, is also not known. What is known is that a supply of yellow bark was purchased during those last weeks. Yellow bark is the ingredient to making quinine, used in treatment of malaria and other fevers.

The mysterious letter Edwards demands of Stephenson prior to his untimely death is fact based. How implicit Stephenson was to this endeavor is again, not known. In the wake of his friend's demise, Edwards faced a Congressional inquest demanding full remittance of the bank's missing assets to the tune of $48,000, a goodly sum in those days amounting to well over $900,000 in today's economy. Edwards, then at political odds with Secretary Crawford, tried to place blame on the man appointing Stephenson both to positions of collecting and overseeing government funds unchecked. He insisted Crawford had received a letter from Stephenson, written under Edwards' direction, stating the conflict of interest. Crawford denied any such letter was received. In order to aid his cause, Edwards' produced a rough draft of a letter, presumed to be in Stephenson's handwriting found among his papers post humously but suspiciously appearing in Edwards' hand. Without any hard evidence on either side, Congress deemed both men to be telling the truth and it was declared inconclusive. Thus both men returned to their respective offices. However, neither fulfilled the future political goals they hoped to achieve.

As indicated, above, the younger Benjamin Stephenson, did indeed venture to California, perhaps with the small ivory miniature in hand as a tribute to his father's legacy and a reminder of his family's prominence in early Illinois. Whether Col. Stephenson ever aspired to push further westward to see the Pacific Ocean or what his thoughts or knowledge of Lewis & Clark's expedition were, is again a vehicle of speculation and creative fiction on this writer's part.

During the early years of their marriage, Ben and Lucy lived right in the pathway where Meriwether Lewis plotted the early stages of the expedition. The couple set up housekeeping in 1803 Harper's Ferry, VA (now WV) where Captain Lewis, around the same time, laid the groundwork for commissioning supplies and scouting out some early recruits. Lucy (Swearingen) Stephenson was born and raised in Wellsburg, WV where one of the men from the Corps of Discovery, Patrick Gass, also lived and served in the militia. For every man chosen there had to have been many who were exempt or couldn't make the trip. Given that the Stephensons were newly married with a child (Julia) born in November 1803, that alone would have made Ben ineligible. Captain Lewis, under President Jefferson's lead, was adamant that only bachelors would be allowed on the dangerous journey into uncharted territory, lest they never return leaving behind widows and orphans.

What is certain is that many Americans waited with bated breath watching the newspapers daily for word on the Corps of Discovery's return. Perhaps that also included Ben and Lucy, who upon the return of the Corps of Discovery in 1807, quickly moved into Kentucky awaiting the official opening of Illinois territory in 1808, having been divided from Indiana. One can almost imagine the elder Ben eagerly perusing the newspapers daily or talking with his social network at the local taverns or after church at a Sunday picnic anticipating new opportunities as the country expanded westward unfettered.

∞∞

There are more stories to tell about the Stephenson family and their adventures in early Illinois territory. Hopefully this one has whet the appetites of those seeking further study on this forgotten part of early American history. It has been quite the adventure for me, writing and living the life of an 1820's house docent. The 1820 Colonel Benjamin Stephenson House is open for public tours Thursday through Saturday 10:00 am to 4:00 pm and Sunday 12:00 to 4:00 pm. Tours are available during those hours with the final tour beginning before 3:00 pm.

 More information on private group tours, events, the community and the Stephenson family are available online at:

http://www.stephensonhouse.org

1820 Colonel Benjamin Stephenson House, Edwardsville, IL
Photos by Maxine Callies

Ninian Edwards,
Territorial Governor of Illinois

5

A HOUSE IN MOURNING

Each October, the Stephenson House honors the life and passing of its founder, Colonel Benjamin Stephenson, with a month long funerary exhibit. Each room depicts a station in the days leading up to and just after the Colonel's death. The parlor is darkened and arranged to depict the laying out of the corpse complete with a period correct wooden coffin. The master bedroom depicts the moment his body was removed after being washed and prepared for burial. Bed linens are askew and bedside tables are littered with medicine bottles and remedies. The dining room portrays the cluttered chaotic days when all household goods were itemized by the lawyer and neatly arrayed on an inventory, ready to be auctioned to pay creditors. It's as if the walls echo the weeping children, hushed orders given by a grieving widow, wondering what life will be like for herself and her children in a far different Illinois than she and her beloved Ben had hoped for. An imaginative visitor might invoke such thoughts while wandering through each room as each stage of that last month with the Colonel is recreated.

One unique artifact that offers a glimpse into those dark days is a poem anonymously posted in *The Edwardsville Spectator*, the newspaper Ben mentions in the story. It is presumed to have been written by the editor and good friend of Ben's, Hooper Warren, who is also mentioned in the story. Though no one is certain who the poet might have been, it is clear it was someone close to the Stephenson family and who was an eye witness to the funeral and happenings. We offer it here for a firsthand glimpse into their world as if you were perusing the paper on October 12, 1822, two days after Benjamin Stephenson's death.

Site director, RoxAnn Raisner,
portraying the Widow Lucy Stephenson
during Mourning Days
Photo by Jill Cook

6

On the Death of Col. Stephenson

An Elegy

The prairies spread with palls of brown,
Their summer's verdant gladness;
And autumn's leaves are fluttering down,
With rustling notes of sadness.

How fled from heaven the cheerful blue,
That decks a sky unclouded;
The aire puts on a dusky hue;
The earth in gloom is shrouded!

Yea, nature seems to mourn with all
Who linger; broken-hearted;
To let the tear of anguish fall,
On dust of friends departed.

But where is he – the just, the good-
Befriending and befriended,
Who firmly for his country-stood,
And to her hail ascended.

I saw him in the summer's ray,
With manly frame unbending;
But ah! Behold yon corse of clay,
A funeral train attending.

I see their sable garbs of woe—
I hear their notes of sorrow;
Which bid the day in darkness flow,
And wean from hope the morrow.

Oh! When he breathed his last farewell,
How wild his orphans' shrieking!
How did her grief, more stifled, tell
Her widow'd heart was breaking!

Insane is woe! By fits, despair
Against the blow is raving;
Or resignation, bending there,
For aid divine is craving.

And may that aid, Almighty God!
Be shed on these, benighted;
And light them from this earthly sod
To where no joys are blighted

(Anonymous poem, presumably by Hooper Warren, editor. Originally published in the Edwardsville Spectator on October 12, 1822, two days after Benjamin Stephenson's death)

7

Bibliography

Matyka, Karen Campe, *Henry the Stephenson House Mouse: A Diary* (2007)

Pease, Theodore, *The Centennial History of Illinois: The Frontier State* (1920)

Edwards, Ninian W., *History of Illinois* (1850)

Wood, Gordon S., *Empire of Liberty: A History of the Early Republic, 1789 – 1815* (2011)

Cather-Wood, Mary Hartwell, *Old Kaskaskia* (1893)

Ferguson, Gillum, *Illinois in the War of 1812* (2012)

Nore, Ellen, *Edwardsville, Illinois, An illustrated history* (1996)

Waller, Elbert, *Illinois Pioneer Days,* (1918)

Duncan, Mildred Owens & Savageau, Mary Duncan, *Tales of Old Settlers of Madison County, Illinois: Stories of the Alton Weekly Telegraph published in Alton,* Illinois (1995)

Jagendorf, M.A., *Sand in the Bag, and other Folktales of Ohio, Indiana and Illinois* (1952)

Tillson, Christiana Holmes, A Woman's Story of Pioneer Illinois (1995)

History of Madison County Illinois 1882

Stepien, Bill & Lewis, Charnelle, *The Illinois Adventure* (1999)

Erichsen-Brown, Charlotte, *Medicinal and Other Uses of North American Plants* (1979)

Baldwin, Carl R., *Captains of the Wilderness* (1986)

Sloane, Eric, *Diary of an Early American Boy* (1962)

8

About the Author

D.L. Andersen has served as a historic docent (interpretive tour guide) at the 1820 Colonel Benjamin Stephenson House since August 2006, about six months after the site opened its doors to the public. She has written articles for the site's newsletters, *The Volunteer* and *The Spectator* as well as a few published short stories, including one for the Agorist Writer's Workshop anthology *Clarion Call II: Echoes of Liberty*. Her historical novel series about the Stephenson Family is slated for publication through Amika Press, Chicago in 2017. She holds a BA in education and music and lives in Southern Illinois with her family, and a menagerie consisting of a cocker spaniel, a rescue dog (terrier-ist), and a cat.

The following pages contain a sneak peak at an upcoming novel series recounting the early years of Ben and Lucy Stephenson before marriage and migration to Illinois territory.

On the Banks of the Ohio

Chapter One

$\mathbb{B}$enjamin Stephenson searched the shadowy woodlands at the edge of the Ohio waiting for Swearingen's woman to arrive. The note was the only reason he'd be staving off a cold winter's eve when there was still work to be done back at the trading post. A ledger awaited his accounting. A new shipment was set to arrive in the next day or two. Supplies were low as winter waned and still several more weeks till planting time. Until then, Farmers would be looking to purchase grain for livestock, staples to stock the larder until kitchen gardens yielded early spring crops.

With spring would come more settlers, looking to make a new start in the Ohio Valley while others pushed onward into the thick forests of the Ohio and Indiana territories to stake their claims in a still as yet unproven and expansive wilderness. For Ben, it meant a new supply of customers to trade goods, or hopefully, spend a few silver or gold coins to increase the business and his own prospects.

The scrap of paper crinkled in his hand, niggling his mind on the possible reasons for her summoning him here.

Met me at Brawker's Riz afer shop cloz, Need tawk.

Ben shook his head and chuckled into the winter stillness, broken only by the wind's whistle through barren trees and the chatter of critters readying another nocturnal hunt. The peripheral sounds tuned his ear while he pondered again the note's meaning. The woman was never one for reading or writing, but that didn't seem to make a difference to her husband. Zack fell under her charms readily enough, her arresting blue eyes and winsome features were reason to turn any man's head, if not for her beguiling form. Dressed up in the finery of an eastern lady, she'd have grace any ballroom with ease. Not that he'd ever been such places. Out here all that mattered was a good woman who could cook, tend a fire, sew and bear a fine lot of sons and daughters to help work the land. If the woman came well dowered with a parcel of land or other property, all the better. Someone to set with of an evening before the fire and read to, discussing ideas both profound and trifling would be more than any man deserved. And if she be a tad easy to gaze upon with a wit to match, was the stuff of idle dreaming.

But he had no use for such trappings at present. His friend may have chosen to fall under a different spell, but he was inured to it all. Those eyes, a fine plump mouth over a dainty chin and a rounded form beneath could be a man's undoing and thus were naught to him.

Ben folded the note and tucked it into his coat pocket. Zack must be ailing again, or he'd have sent word himself or paid a call at the shop, unless he was still stewing over their last quarrel. Ben jerked off a glove and scratched ink stained fingers against his bristly chin. It wasn't like Zack to be so pigheaded and contrary. He should have called on his friend long before now. But there had been other matters to settle, promises to keep, always another promise to honor and a favor to return. It was all good business and being neighborly.

He leaned on the barrel of his long gun and looked impatiently about the silent trees towering above him in endless supplication to the sky. Or were they brooding over him as if to wonder why he should be sitting so still, alone, gun locked with barrel to the heavens and yet not take from the forests another life to fill the bellies of some settler's family or scavenge a pelt to grace some strutting eastern gentleman or fine English lady across the great sea. He should check on a few traps while he was here, before heading back to the store. She better come soon, he thought as he kicked the snow off the fallen log to ready a place to sit.

A mist became a shadow against the thickness of a gnarled elm, undulating with and against the tall trunks standing sentinel. A trick of the eye, he thought. Couldn't be what he just thought he saw. Not in these woods. But still, his hand twitched, easing the flintlock ready to aim. He could shoot the feather off a sparrow's tail if he had to, but this was no sparrow. His sinewy arms strained beneath the layers of linen and wool. His face hardened into keen awareness of every sound, every footfall and snap of twig. Could be nothing more than a flit of a jay, the glint of the sun's last whisper through the barren trees before falling into shadow.

"Ben." The small voice, barely a whisper from the opposite direction, wafted through the crisp winter air like breath on frosted windowpane. He turned to see Phoebe standing a few feet away; her slave followed a pace behind with downcast eyes, just enough to show her submission but the stubborn jut of her chin spoke otherwise. Both women staved off winter's chill swathed in woolen shawls and hooded cloaks. Phoebe's eyes sparkled against rosy cheeks illuminated in the milky softness of the setting sun.

"I thank'ee for comin' out here like this." She bit her lip and took a step forward. "I didna keep ya waitin' long."

"No, not long." Ben stepped over the dead log and offered a hand to help Phoebe gain her footing. "What's this all about?" His voice sounded far pleasanter than he felt, though curiosity grew like a weed in his bosom.

Her gloved hand gripped firmly in his as one narrow boot landed over a tangle of frosted roots. She looked back to the slave girl gazing warily around the thicket.

"Achsa, you best go on now and see if any o' them sugar maples is gettin' ready for tappin."

"But Mizz Phoebe, we done checked them t'other day and…"

"Just do as I say, girl, y'hear?" She turned blinking eyes at Ben. "Mr. Stephenson and I…. Have some matters to discuss."

"Yas'm." The girl raised a sidelong glance before trudging off, one heavy foot at a time through the snow covered trees.

Phoebe turned again to her slave one last time. "And don't ya'll come poking back here until I come to fech ya'll, y'hear?"

"Yas'm."

Ben kept his eyes peeled between the two women, waiting for Achsa to disappear into the densely packed trees. His initial attempt at conversation was met with Phoebe's lifted finger and a flash to be still.

"Now, What's all this about, Phoebe? Is Zack-?"

"I didn't know any other way to speak to you without..." Phoebe tugged on the fringe of her shawl, looked around as if searching for some sign of danger lurking behind every darkened tree. "Things, they ain't good. Figured you oughta know, is all." She folded her arms, pulling the wool wrap in a tight caress across her shoulders beneath the woolen cloak. "He's talking crazy these days. I thought you'd be comin' round again. I know you had your words the last time, but it weren't his fault, what he said."

"Phoebe, I bear him no malice. We just... had a difference of opinion. I've had too much going on at the shop..."

She flashed a look of watery fire at him. She was not above crying to get her way. He hated to see a woman cry, but this seemed more than mere feminine wiles.

"What is it, Phoebe?" he sat down on the log and brushed a place for her.

"No one's been by, which is fine on account o' Zack... He don't want no one to know... not just yet... not even his folks."

Ben studied the trees, taller now as he sat beneath them near the forest floor, the smell of decaying lichen against the raw cold of winter. "Then it's begun again? The fevers? It's no different than last time."

"It be different. Worse now than last harvest time." Her voice broke through the stillness like the crack of an ice laden branch. "I been hoping he'll get better. But hopin' don't change nothing."

"Bilious fever," Ben muttered, "It comes and goes. Most everyone's had the ague at one time or other."

She shook her head, her lower lip trembled and then steeled into a firm line. "This ain't no regular ague. I seen it afore when it get this bad. Once. I oughta knowed. I did know… And still I took to marry him, 'cause I thought there'd be time. It'd all work out all right."

"Time?" Ben asked, though more to himself than her. He suspected what she meant. He and Zack had argued about it. The lawsuit. The land claim. Perhaps in the man's illness, he'd lay it to rest. It was one small tract of land among hundreds the Swearingens owned.

Shepherd's back in these parts, Ben. It's up to us now to make it right. You understand?

Indeed he had understood, though he yet resisted that day Zack laid out his plan. He recalled his friend's pensive agitation even in his usual amiable manner. A hint of sweat on his brow and a tremble to his hand as he quaffed his whiskey.

"There's no use fretting over it now." Phoebe sat a bit too close for comfort, or was that precisely the reason? With the setting sun came a deepening chill, he should get them both to shelter soon.

"You won't have to go through this alone, Phoebe." Ben spoke softly, carefully, his view on their mingled cloudy breath dissipating into the trees. "I should've come by sooner and made everything right."

She shot piercing blue eyes at him. "Aye, ya should'a done a lot o' things different. We all should'a. But no use fretting over milk what's been spilt on the barn floor."

"I'll take you home now. Fetch your slave girl and we'll get you both out of this cold." He stood with hand ready to take her arm.

"No, not till I say my peace." She rose, slipping free of his aid and placed a hand on a nearby sycamore, picking at the bark. "He'll be dead afore long." The corner of her mouth snaked into a wan smile. "There I said it. Haven't wanted to think on it, but it's said. Not even married one full year and already a widder woman." She snorted, worrying a lower lip tight against teeth. "Best get used to wearin' black bombazine."

Ben drew toward her, stunned as if she'd slapped him. "Phoebe, let's not talk about this now." He lifted a comforting hand toward the back of her hood, then let it drop to his side when she turned abruptly.

"I got to know what will happen to his land, his property. Will it all be mine?"

She slithered the strips of shorn bark through her fingers, letting them rain onto the ground. The bare patch on the tree lay naked, raw.

"Lass, you can't think on that now."

Acid burned his stomach. Her words still stung, though they bore truth, but this was no time to discuss land rights.

"I got to know." She curled her hand into a fist and pounded the tree. "They won't take it back. His family, and now that Newhouse."

"No one's going to take anything away. You're entitled to everything he has by law. Who's telling you this?" A cold wind blew down from the north. He knew what she feared, though he still found the notion as delirious as his fevered friend's behavior must be. "Did Zack send you out here? We'll go see him now. I could have come to the house."

She shook her head, brooding into the distance. Her pale lashes lay in a soft curve against the line of her gently rounded cheek. "He don't know I'm here. This is the best way. Of late, he don't know much of anything, where I go or even who I am most days. Just keeps saying he's got to set all to right. Keeps reliving things that should be dead and gone. Fights Injuns in his sleep." She lowered her hood, causing Ben's next breath to seize at the base of his throat. A bruise, the mark of a man's balm colored her neck.

"Did Zack do this?" Ben whispered, incredulously.

"He didn't mean to. It's the way o' that damned fever when it gets real bad. It was the other night. Him fightin' Injuns again... he didn't mean it." She removed a glove and tenderly traced the bruise.

"We'll keep him tied down. It's the only way. A dose of laudanum will..."

She breathed a wan smile. "You doctorin' now as well as lawyerin' and surveyin'? Got all the answers don't ya. We been trying to keep him tied down. Me and Ansel and the other manservants. I just can't do it no more."

58

"I'll stay with you both and help look after him, or fetch the barber from Wheeling for a physick."

"I got to know." She curled her hand into a fist and pounded the tree. "They won't take it back. His folk, and now that Newhouse, can't take it all away from me... from us?" Her voice was unsettling, her gaze fixed, disquiet when she said, 'us'. She had to mean her and her husband, though something belied that.

"No one's going to take anything away that is rightfully yours. You're both entitled to everything he has by law. Where you getting this?"

"The land, he keeps sayin' things I can't believe be true. I know you had some dealings worked out 'twixt you."

What had Zack been telling her? Or was this the handiwork of another? "Only thing I done is help him with a few legal matters. Pointed him in the right direction of the law and land rights. The rest is up to a court to decide."

"Then you get my meaning," she said, "I do know what's in the old man's will for you. He put you in there didn't he? All fine and proper like, I hear. You was like a son to him."

"It's not that simple, Phoebe." *Even for me*, he started to say, but thought the better and was soon interrupted.

"I'd a said yes, if'n you'd asked me... afore Zack did." She swallowed a sharp breath and blinked coyly. "Even without no land or fortune."

Ben set his jaw, forcing back a chuckle. "I don't recall askin' nor did I have a mind to."

A brief glimmer, desperate and pained, marred her lovely face, almost as if he too had struck her. She lifted her chin into a mask of fierce determination.

Ben softened into an even tone. "You were better off with Zack, you know this. I've got other plans that don't include…"

"Better off, am I?" she said. "I remember how fine you looked on Public Day three year ago. All dandied out in your new roundabout and waistcoat when you asked me to dance. I wondered then what it'd be like to dance with you, to… do other things to… I reckon."

He shrugged and lifted from their perch to move his frozen feet. "I got my own plans. Don't be holding on to things that make no difference now."

She worked her jaw sardonically. "Oh, I know what plans you got. It's all in the old man's will, ain't it? The fine and noble Captain Andrew Van Swearingen, Injun Fighter of the Ohio Valley. But I know what you gotta do to get that choice piece of land and a stake in his fortune."

"I never said-"

"He bought you body and soul, just like he done the rest of us, or any one of his slaves. A fine lot they are, them Swearingens, ain't they? My Zechariah was the only decent one of the whole litter. Elzey is nothin' more than roustabout who don't care a stitch for the land, but sure can drink and rut his way through the money reaped from it. Drusilla she got herself all set now, even if she be a widder too. The fine Mrs. Brady, still got her land and her husband's reputation to back her up, along with her dead Pappy."

"Phoebe, enough!"

"Then there's them three young 'uns, but you're watchin' out for them now, ain't ya? Got your reasons too. Don't think I don't know it. That part of your plan?"

"Phoebe, what's this about?" Ben returned to the sycamore tree an laid a hand against hers to still her incessant fidgeting of the tree bark. "Please, don't do this now."

60

"So, I'm asking," she said, turning as if not even hearing him. "Can they truly take it from me, if'n there be no heirs from Zack? That's all I need to know."

Ben took a step back and swiped a hand down his face. In the waning afternoon sun, pale wisps glowed from under her bonnet. Her rosy mouth panted curls of warm breath into the chilling evening air. He thought carefully what more to tell her. "When the time comes... if it does - and hopefully not for many years - you will be entitled to something. You won't be left destitute. There are legal provisions for widows, with or without heirs. As far as I reckon probates, and the law... though it's been some time..."

"But I won't get it all, will I?" She clenched her fists firm against her ribs and strode away. "The land, the slaves and even the fine things in my house, they all go back don't they? I get the slave girl, Achsa - she was a wedding gift - and the money we been saving and that's about all."

"You are entitled to keep the house, a place to live, at least, and a one-third dower's portion as befits the law. I'm sorry, Phoebe, I don't see..." Ben shook his head, incredulous at what he was hearing. His friend faced a horrific death, slow, insidiously painful and debilitating. And this woman stood fretting over a few acres of land and some family baubles. How much had she worried Zack with this nonsense? "I think it best we get you home and see to your husband. Who is with him now?"

Phoebe clasped hands beneath her chin and seemed not to hear him at first. "Big Ansel. He'll keep him contained till I get back. We got to settle this here and now, before it's too late."

"We can settle this easy enough back at your cabin."

"I tried to speak with Zechariah on all this, but it's no use. He keeps fretting over those little ones. They's only his half-blood kin, two brothers and a sister. Dotes on 'em like they's his own, especially that baby sister. He says he wants her to have the Dutch lady. Keeps asking me to give it to her, but I don't know where he hid it. Worth a king's ransom, they say. I only wore it once, the day we wed." Slender fingers played at the hollow of her collarbone, inches from the thumb size bruise circling her neck like fiendish purple ribbon. "Everyone said I looked prettier than any courtly lady."

Ben stood silent, listening, not certain what to say to this woman here in the middle of the forest. "Phoebe, Zack will need you to be strong in the days to come. This isn't him." He grazed a finger to her neck. Just know that he would never, in his right mind do such a thing, not to you nor any woman."

She turned on him with the sharp look of a cornered cat, grasping his hand into the curve of her throat. Charmingly, she softened into a bewildered smile as she slumped against the tree, pulling him with her. "He'll write no will, if that's what you're aiming at. That's a certainty. I done asked him already."

"I'll do what I can to help." Ben remained there pinned with her against the tree, too close. He stood entirely too close, but she had been hurt, needed comfort. He wanted to help, but in her state, he wasn't sure the woman should be entitled to anything in the way of Swearingen fortune. "There would be provisions for you, if a will were properly drawn. A judge might rule in your favor and you'd get at least a decent size tract to call your own. There's another possibility as well, a recounting of the Captain's will, certain land tracts can be disputed…"

She snorted and shook her head letting it loll back against the frozen trunk. "Dead these five years now, and still the old Captain's got his hold on us all." She flashed steely eyes that sent a disturbing blast through him. "I trust in you, Ben. You'll do right by me, by us. I knew you would."

Ben again wasn't sure who she meant by 'us' but easily dismissed it as befitting a marriage bond. Yes, he'd help her, and Zechariah, his friend, as her husband. He pulled free of her hand trailing awkwardly down the bodice of her gown, allowing him to feel her warmth, her every curve.

Pacing to the old log, he formed his thoughts and sat down to broach the subject next on his mind. *Shepherd's back in these parts.*

"Phoebe, has Zack said anything about a man named Abraham Shepherd?" He studied her for any sign of recollection but she only leaned against the tree, gazing at some indistinct point. Could she be seeing what he sensed earlier, hidden there among the shadowy branches and snow capped trunks? His musket was still within easy reach.

"Shepherd. Yes, I know about that man. It's all he's been talking about. How he's got to protect them little ones. Van, Lucy, Tommy. That's all that matters. And likely it be John Newhouse behind it all. Nelly should a never wed him. Can't say I blame her, though." She angled her head toward him and sauntered over to the log. "Old Injun Van sure be rolling in his grave knowing a man like that is taking to his bed. Zack 'ud a took them three young 'uns in to live with us, when Eleanor wed last fall, but they's better off with their Mama, even with the likes of a step-pappy like him. She blinked, pressing her mouth into a thin line. Unlatching her cloak, she let it fall free to the forest floor; her shawl sank in soft folds to the crook of her arms.

"Ben, you could write Zack's will for him. You know the legal way. All he'd need do is make his mark on it. You could help him with that as well. The way he's been lately, he won't know no different." She leaned over him, her eyes gleaming with a wild hopefulness that disquieted him further.

"I won't do that. I'm not a proper lawyer. It damn sure wouldn't be legal." He had only told her a little lie. A man didn't need to pass the bar to write a will. He could even do this for himself with only a witness to sign and vouch for it. But she didn't need to hear that from him. He would not lie for her. Would she be determined enough to find someone who would?

"Then I know of only one other way." She dug a toe into a snowy patch, mingling the dirt beneath with the crunched ice cap.

"A way out for us… all of us, including the young 'uns." She took a long ragged breath and sat down beside him on the log, her sapphire eyes piercing with determined desperation. "If'n the only way to get the entire fortune is by blood, then…. Ben-" A swallow of cold air drew the steamy breath back behind teeth pearled over a soft rosy mouth. "I got to have a babe, an heir for Zack. But I fear there ain't time afore… He can't… I mean… he shouldn't. Any child he beget now mightn't be right." She poked a finger at her temple.

"Phoebe what's your meaning?" Ben paused to consider her words. "It's utter nonsense… ignorant superstition." He retreated but she followed as a shadow at his heels. "Let's get you back home now. Call your girl back. Achsa is it?"

"Tis so. I heard such as this. I seen the hydrophoby when I was young, back in Pinkney Creek. I know what it can do. This ain't no different and can leave a man's seed tainted." She pressed her lips together, a crease formed between her eyes darkening the sapphire orbs to a midnight sky. "But if'n someone else was to get a baby for Zack, someone close to him, so's he wouldn't mind… not that he need know… nor anyone else neither."

Ben locked his knees and tried to breath in even strokes. "You can't possibly mean… What have you done, Phoebe? Who? Who is he?" Ben grabbed his gun, still set against the hickory trunk near the log. He pondered the purple trace around her neck. Was that indeed Zack's doing? Or had there been another? "Who is he, Phoebe? What are you telling me?" With this new information came rage, confusion and a host of images he steeled against.

"I done nothing… yet, that is." She withdrew and then gentled her fingers against his grip on the steel barrel of his long gun. "I know you'd help me… help Zack… us… and we'd… we'd make it all work out right."

Realization flooded over Ben with sickening presentiment. "No... hell no. You're madder than a hatter. Let's get you home, Mrs. Swearingen. Your husband has need of you, of us. His wife and his friend."

Phoebe eased closer, her hand tapped lightly on the barrel's muzzle before coursing gently in ascent to his woolen sleeve. For a moment she cast a desperate wild look into the forest and swayed. Ben steadied her with a hand at her elbow, fearing she'd faint, while trying to aim her toward the path out of the woods.

She resisted and leaned into him, her face inches from his. "You'll help me, then? We'll make a babe for Zack and everything will be all right." She spoke more as if to herself, reassuring against a plan too dastardly even for her to consider.

Ben stroked her rosy cheek with the back of his bare fingers and gritted his teeth. A scent of lilac and wisteria feathered across the tip of his nose, curling into the ridges and cavity between his cheekbones. Five-and-a-half pennies per ounce for Eastern toilet water. A full four ounce bottle at the store could set a man back just under two bits, same price as a small ax. Either, well applied could tear a man asunder. She must mean business to wash herself in fine cologne just to come traipsing in the winter woods to sell her wares.

"No," he said, "I don't intend to stay here in these parts long, you know that. I don't need anything tying me here, least not you and some kid you'll pass off as some other man's." He spoke in a low gentle tone hoping it would be enough to appease her. It took every fiber of control not to grab and shake such an insidious notion from her devilish mind. He bit his lip to keep from calling her every filthy name reserved only for tavern maids. No, she was worse than that, for even the tavern wench earned her own bread, upfront and honest rather than by deception.

She pulled away, never taking her penetrating gaze from him. "I know about Old Swearingen's will. He done his part by you, didn't he? Set you up right fine, he did. Almost like you was his son too." She laid a trembling hand on his arm while she reached to unpin her bodice front. "That's why this could work. You'll see. It'll be Zack's baby, but ours too. You don't even need to stay around if'n you don't want to."

"I said no." He backed away, and retrieved her cloak, still lying on the frozen ground. "Now with or without you, I'm heading over to see Zack." He placed the cloak around her shoulders; she flinched away, but then accepted its warmth.

"She ain't even bleedin' age yet." Phoebe spun around, her face skewed in anger. "Won't be for nigh on three, maybe four year or more. You don't have to wait that long, or maybe you want to, but even still you could have-"

"Enough!" His shout reverberated off the trees, startling a pair of cardinals to a higher limb of the sycamore. "There's more to consider here. Just give me some time on this and I'll come up with something. You know Shepherd's back and ready to make trouble again."

She straightened her shawl beneath her cloak, calmer now, staring at the frozen ground. "And now that Zack is... he can't pursue the legal way no more."

"Yes... maybe..." He spread his hands in helpless exasperation. "I don't know just yet." His head throbbed and his chest pounded with notions entering his mind that had no place there. The pins of her gown, to easy to undo. They were alone. She had told her slave girl not to return until called. Lilac and wisteria. He had to get away from here. He paced further into the thicket wondering just how to deal with this hysterical woman, a diseased friend and now the certainty of what would transpire in the weeks to come. There were others to consider here as well. But he couldn't think on all that just yet.

He rounded on her with pointed finger. "Who is telling you all of this? Giving you such notions?" Ben had an idea but wanted to hear it from her first.

"It's what the old man's will say. I know how they feel about me, how they've always felt. Them Swearingens think they so high and mighty. The old man always did say they come from Dutch noblemen stock." Her voice broke as she turned to lean against the sycamore again, clenching fists at her side.

"He'd never allowed Zack to marry someone like me, someone who come from…" A baleful laugh filled the unspoken gap. "He give his own bastards a claim, but not his lawful son's wife. No heir, no land claim."

"I'm going back to see Zechariah now, Mrs. Swearingen." Ben headed toward her cautiously, hoping she'd not try any more tricks. He didn't want to leave her here but would if she refused to follow.

She slumped against the tree, as if drawing one last ounce of strength, and then rose to full height, a mad cold resolve lighting her face in the soft glow of eventide. "I'll get me a babe for Zack, one way or another, I will. Whether it be you or someone else. I will, I tell you. And I'll not leave my land."

It was the scream of a panther in the distance that drove her to him. Or had it been her own cry of anger, desperation? It frightened her, startled him. She was cold, needed comfort. He only meant a momentary embrace, reassuring, shielding. In the dusk, she felt warm in his arms. The cover of darkness surrounded them, a mist settling into the creases of night, shadow and wilderness sheltering them from sight, sound, a place where no one need know. He kissed her full, deep. Or she kissed him. Did it matter? He should cease. Push her away.

"Mizz Phoebe?" Achsa stood trembling on the path. "I know ya'll said to wait, but it be gettin' mighty late now. I thought I heard a wolf howl over yonder. Beggin' your pardon, Ma'am… Mr. Stephenson, sir, but shouldn't we be gettin' home now?"

Ben eased her back against the tree, took a deep swig of cold cleansing air and said, "Yes, right you are, Achsa. Mrs. Swearingen was just saying about the same thing. I'll see you two back to the main road and come back and see about that wolf."

Also by D.L. Andersen

(coming soon)

The Stephenson House Chronicles:

On the Banks of the Ohio

That Far Distant Country

The Goshen Road

∞∞∞∞∞

Novellas:

A Stephenson Steampunk

A Stephenson House Christmas

For more information on upcoming books visit with the author online on Facebook, Twitter, Good Reads and Amazon author pages.

Made in the USA
San Bernardino, CA
27 September 2016